Experiencing God's Love
A Guide for New Believers

Unless otherwise indicated, all scripture quotations are taken from the *King James Version* of the Bible.

Scripture quotations marked *AMP* are taken from *The Amplified Bible, Old Testament,* Copyright © 1965, 1987 by the Zondervan Corporation. *The Amplified New Testament,* Copyright ©1958, 1987 by The Lockman Foundation. Used by permission.

Scripture quotations marked *NKJV* are taken from the *New King James Version* of the Bible. Copyright © 1979, 1980, 1982 by Thomas Nelson, Inc. Used by permission. All rights reserved.

Experiencing God's Love – A Guide for New Believers
1-59089-806-0
©2003 by Dr. Creflo A. Dollar
Creflo Dollar Ministries
P.O. Box 490124
College Park, GA 30349

Published by:
Creflo Dollar Publications
P.O. Box 490124
College Park, GA 30349

Printed in the United States of America.

Contents

Introduction

Welcome to the family of God! From this point forward, your life will *never* be the same again. Deciding to turn your life over to Jesus Christ is the best decision you could ever make. You have taken a step in the right direction, and you won't regret it.

Years ago, my decision to finally surrender my life to the Lord put me on the road to a better existence. I am who I am today because I was smart enough to allow Him to take control of my life. Each of us has a story to share about who we are, what we've experienced and the kind of life we would like to live. But the most important aspect about our lives should be where God fits into the picture. That is what Christianity is all about—accepting the need for God's influence in our lives and allowing Him to lead us down the road to a better life.

While on your journey, expect to learn things about God that will compel you to love Him with all your heart and soul. Expect to mature spiritually and become a better person. I have come to learn that *expectation* is a key to success. What you *expect* out of life is what you will *experience*. What you expect from your relationship with God is vital; therefore, expect nothing less than to experience *all* of the good things that He has in store for you.

Allow me to clarify something. I am not promising you that life will be a bed of roses now that you're a Christian. Others may have told you, "Everything's going to be all right now!" But the truth is that life has its challenges, and adversity *will* come; however, the way in which you respond to troubling situations makes all the difference.

As a new believer, you can be confident that God has provided you with the proper "equipment" so that you can win big in life despite the challenges that will come your way. You can either allow them to throw you off course, or you can use them as opportunities to succeed. The temptation to give in to the pressures of life will be intense; however, do as I have done: learn to stand strong when the pressure is on.

I can't tell you the number of times in the past that I was tempted to quit Christianity altogether and return to my old lifestyle of drinking, cursing and fornicating. Back then I was not serious about being what I call "for real saved." I was distracted by my own agenda and almost took a costly detour from the path that God had designed for me.

My reason for writing this book is to help you to stay on the course that God has designed for you. Therefore, I would like to briefly share with you several key steps that are guaranteed to keep you on the right track. I am convinced that these are the *complete* steps to salvation. I have come to realize that many well-meaning Christians don't know that there is a process to being born again. They assume that a person simply needs to believe in Jesus and that that decision will automatically make them a "born-again Christian." It does not work that way. Later in this book I will discuss in detail what *salvation* and being *born again* mean. For now, allow me to list the steps to complete salvation and their corresponding biblical references.

1. Recognize and admit that you are a sinner (Psalm 51:5).

2. Repent of your sins (1 John 1:9).

3. Confess Jesus as your Lord (Romans 10:9-10).

4. Baptism in water and Baptism of the Holy Spirit with the evidence of speaking in tongues (Matthew 3:6; Acts 2:3-4, 38; Acts 8:14, 17).

5. Obey the Word of God (1 John 5:3).

Your following these steps does not mean that it will be easy sailing from now on. You still have a responsibility to continue growing and maturing into spiritual adulthood. At this point, you may be eager to serve God and are not afraid to share your newfound faith with others. That's wonderful! However, the key to maintaining that fervor is to *discipline* yourself to live as God intends. Discipline will help you to remain focused on fulfilling His plan for your life. That is my heartfelt desire for all believers—to help people understand and experience the essence of Who God is and to obtain all that He has in store for them. Helping people to know Him intimately thrills me!

There is a great need for you to know God personally. Simply knowing *about* Him is not enough. There are many people who claim to know Him, but they really don't *know* Him. I encourage you to strive to be someone who does not see Him as just a "Higher Power" or the "Supreme Being" of the universe. He is so much more than that; He is your heavenly *Father*. As is the case with any parent, He wants the best for you. He wants you to dream big and then use His assistance to fulfill your dreams. He wants to provide for your every need. God wants to laugh with you, comfort you when you're down, be there for you when you're lonely, strengthen you when you're weak—you name it, He wants to be your everything!

This is the God I hope you come to know, love, honor and respect. This will happen the more you work to develop an intimate relationship with Him. Drawing closer to your heavenly Father daily should be your heart's desire and mission in life. Keep in mind that to experience a close-knit relationship with Him is to experience His love, and to experience His love is to experience all that He is. Now that's worth living for!

Dr. Creflo A. Dollar

Dr. Creflo A. Dollar

Chapter 1
All for Love

1

≈

All for Love

Years ago I wrote a book titled, *Lord Teach Me How to Love*. In it I share my testimony of how the love of God changed my life forever. Something happens to people when they're "touched" by His love. They no longer see life as they used to. Their attitudes and mindsets change, and they begin to appreciate God for all that He has done, is doing and will do for them.

I'll never forget the time when a friend invited me to a home Bible study shortly after I became born again. He was mentoring me in how to live the lifestyle of a Christian. As soon as I walked into the apartment where the Bible study was held, all 12 people quickly stood to welcome me. They hugged me and told me how much they appreciated my being there. Those people didn't know me, but that didn't stop them from showing love to me. Their demonstration of love and acceptance is what prompted me to continue attending that Bible study.

I am sure that you have a personal story of how God's love compelled you to give your life over to Him. I encourage you to keep that inner fire burning as you mature in your Christian walk. Always keep in the forefront of your mind how much the Lord loves you. Remember that He loves you too much to abandon you, too much not to provide for your needs and too much not to protect you. That's the kind of God for Whom you are now living, He is a God of love!

Love Has a Purpose

Perhaps you have heard a lot about God's love. You may have seen the words "JOHN 3:16" displayed at ballgames, on church marquees or on billboards along the highway. Have you ever wondered what it means? One thing is for sure: it is not just a catchy slogan. In *The Amplified Bible* translation, it is a biblical reference that reads,

> "For **God so greatly loved and dearly prized the world,** that He [even] gave up His only begotten (unique) Son, so that whoever believes in (trusts in, clings to, relies on) Him shall not perish (come to destruction, be lost) but have eternal (everlasting) life."

First, notice that this scripture talks about the abundance of God's love for the world. The word *world* here is a reference to "people," not the physical planet in which we live. God loves *all* people, even those who reject Him and do all sorts of ungodly things. The reason He is able to love everyone despite their shortcomings is that He is incapable of hating His creation. In fact, hate does not exist in Him, only love does. A better way to see this love is by replacing the words "the world" with your name. For example:

*"For **God so greatly loved and dearly prized Creflo,** that He [even] gave up His only begotten (unique) Son, so that whoever believes in (trusts in, clings to, relies on) Him shall not perish (come to destruction, be lost) but have eternal (everlasting) life."*

Have you ever attempted to define what *love* is? Perhaps you have thought that it is just an emotion; a strong "feeling" you develop over time when you're romantically involved with someone. Love is much more than that. I have come to learn that *what* love is is not as important as *Who* love is. To begin understanding the love of God, I encourage you to read the three epistles, or letters, that the Apostle John wrote to the body of Christ (Christians). These letters, First, Second and Third John, are powerful in their simplicity and clarity.

In 1 John 4:16, the *New King James Version,* John writes, *"And we have known and believed the love that God has for us. God is love; and he who abides in love abides in God, and God in him."* Did you get that? God *is* love; He doesn't just *have* love. This makes sense when you think about it. Everything that God does on your behalf is an act of His love. His protection is an act of His love. His provision for your needs is an act of His love. Not only that, His acceptance of you into His family is done out of love; therefore, you can call Him Father, or "Daddy" (Romans 8:15, *AMP;* Galatians 4:6, *AMP*).

Now you see why John 3:16 is such a powerful scripture. It addresses the extreme length that God went to to express His love (Himself) for you. He loves you so much that He can't stand to be separated from you spiritually or otherwise. His original plan was to create mankind (men and women) for fellowship and a relationship with Him.

Separated, But Not Out of Reach

In reading through Genesis 2-3, it becomes clear that the Lord first prepared a great paradise—the earth—with everything anyone could possibly desire. Paradise was God's gift to man. Psalm 115:16 says, *"The heaven, even the heavens, are the Lord's: but the earth hath he given to the children of men."*

Paradise had it all: from great beauty, sumptuous food, vast lands and precious gems to gold, silver and a variety of animals of all shapes and sizes. God put this in place in preparation for and anticipation of His greatest creation—mankind. Then He created Adam and Eve, placed them within this wonderful paradise and gave them free access to fellowship with Him intimately. And because He did not want them to be puppets or robots, He endowed them with a free will to either choose to rebel or to walk forever with Him.

Unfortunately, Adam made a fatal choice: He disobeyed the Lord and suffered the consequences—physical and spiritual separation from Him. The Lord had given Adam every blessing imaginable with only the simplest of instructions. It's like giving your child the okay to play outside just as long as he or she obeys your rules.

Genesis 2:15-17 makes God's instructions to Adam very clear:

And the Lord God took the man, and put him into the garden of Eden to dress it and to keep it. And the Lord God commanded the man, saying, Of every tree of the garden thou mayest freely eat: But of the tree of the knowledge of good and evil, thou shalt not eat of it: for in the day that thou eatest thereof thou shalt surely die.

In simple terms, Adam was instructed to: (1) *keep* the garden, or "to guard; garrison about; protect" it; (2) to eat freely of all of the trees of the garden except one and (3) to not eat of the tree of the knowledge of good and evil.

Satan, disguised as a serpent, chose to approach *Eve* to deceive her into disobeying God's instructions. Unfortunately, Eve allowed herself to be deceived by the serpent's lie that God was trying to keep them from being like Him. The truth was, Adam and Eve were *already* like God, made in His image and endowed with the same character. In addition, Adam knew exactly what the Father had said. He was with Eve while the serpent was tempting her, but chose to remain silent. Remember, it was Adam's job to protect the garden as God had instructed. If he had, the Devil would not have been able to invade paradise and deceive his wife.

The point I am trying to make is that Adam could have chosen not to disobey God; unfortunately, he chose his own way over God's (Genesis 3:1-6). Adam's disobedience and rebellion separated mankind from God. This was a separation from Love Himself and His protection. It's like a newborn being snatched away from its parents, and that child growing up not knowing its natural mother and father.

That's what happened to mankind when Adam sinned (messed up, missed the mark). He opened the door to the consequences of his disobedience—spiritual separation from God, sickness, lust, greed, anger, bitterness, depression, jealousy and so on—and closed the door to God's love. Romans 5:12 says, *"Wherefore, as by one man [Adam] sin entered into the world, and death by sin and so death passed upon all men, for that all have sinned."* According to this scripture, death also entered the world along with sin. You have to understand that before Adam's "fall," neither he nor Eve could die. Their physical bodies were created to live forever.

It is also important to note that *death* is defined as "separation from life." Ephesians 4:17-18 tells us that people who have not given their lives over to God are alienated from the *life of God—the* source that gives them eternal life with Him. Therefore, when Adam sinned, he alienated himself from life with God, and spiritual death was the result.

The "sin" that Romans 5:12 refers to has little to do with Adam having done something "bad." When a person commits an *act* of sin, he or she simply "misses the mark." What mark? The mark, or standard, of godly living. Adam's sin caused him to change his godly *state of being* to a sinful one. When God created him, Adam's state of being was sinless and indestructible. But the moment Adam, God's son (Luke 3:38), ate the forbidden fruit, he took on the nature of sin. He died spiritually and began to die physically. A spiritually dead person has no connection, or relationship, with the Lord, and his or her life is destined for eternal separation from the life of God.

How many of us would quickly give up on someone if he or she turned his or her back on us? Our human nature tends to ostracize those who do something against us. I am glad that *God's* nature isn't like that. When Adam sinned against Him, the Father made a decision to love him anyway. He could have wiped Adam and Eve off the face of earth and start over, but He didn't. His love for them compelled Him to develop a plan for man to be reconciled, or rejoined, to Him. That's where Jesus comes in.

First Corinthians 15:21-22 says that despite the fact that a man allowed sin to enter the earth, God would use another Man to reverse the effects of sin and death. Verse 22 says, *"For as in Adam all die, even so in Christ [Jesus] shall all men be made alive."* The process of "making man alive" refers to God's plan for giving mankind a solution whereby they could exchange their sinful state of being for a godly one. Through Jesus, man can regain the life of God and *live* again. You see, before you were made alive through Christ, you were "dead" in your sins and separated from the heavenly Father. Ephesians 2:1-2 *(AMP)* makes this point clear:

And you [He made alive], when you were dead (slain) by [your] trespasses and sins in which at one time you walked [habitually]. You were following the course and fashion of this world [were under the sway of the tendency of this present age], following the prince of the power of the air. [You were obedient to and under the control of] the [demon] spirit that stills constantly works in the sons of disobedience [the careless, the rebellious, and the unbelieving, who go against the purposes of God].

You can't get any plainer and more straightforward than that. When you were in your "sin state," you were under Satan's influence. This may sound harsh to you, but it's true. When God isn't your "pilot," as some people say, Satan is. The Devil's plan is to control and manipulate people and keep them from living for God. Aren't you glad that you fired the Devil and hired the Lord to take control of your life? Your decision was an acceptance of the Father's great love for you. You accepted the fact that Jesus is the way to restore your relationship with your heavenly Father (John 14:6).

In the Flesh

Now, think back to John 3:16 and what it says concerning the great sacrifice that God made for you and your relationship with Him. He loves you so much that He came to this world Himself in the flesh, or in bodily form (John 1:1-14; 1 Timothy 3:16). Many people become puzzled when they learn about God's physical manifestation, or appearance as Jesus. But the prophet Isaiah gave us insight into the fact that Jesus was God in the flesh: *"Therefore the Lord himself shall give you a sign; Behold, a virgin shall conceive, and bear a son, and shall call his name Immanuel"* (Isaiah 7:14). Matthew echoed this prophecy and let us know the Hebrew word *Immanuel* (or *Emmanuel)* is translated, "God with us" (Matthew 1:22-23). The writer of Hebrews wrote, *"...unto the Son he saith, Thy throne, **O God,** is for ever and ever: a sceptre of righteousness is the sceptre of thy kingdom"* (Hebrews 1:8). Second Corinthians 5:19 clearly states that "God was in Christ." And John 1:1-3 *(NKJV)* says, *"In the beginning was the Word [Jesus], and the Word was with God, and **the Word was God.** He was in the beginning with God. All things were made through Him, and without Him nothing was made that was made."*

Based on these scriptures, there is no doubt that God's love for us is so great that He *chose* to come to the earth for our benefit. He, as Jesus, experienced all of the challenges, temptations and trials that you could ever face in this lifetime. It was His assurance to you that He can relate to and sympathize with *whatever* you experience in life (Hebrews 4:15-16, *AMP).* That's love!

The Father's willingness to express His love for you should make you want to shout and dance! You can rejoice knowing that He loves you as much as He loves Jesus (John 17:23). Allow me to repeat that: Your heavenly Father loves you *as much as* He loves Jesus. The Bible says that Jesus is His "beloved" (Luke 3:22). That means *you* are the Father's beloved son or daughter. John 5:20 in *The Amplified Bible* says that the Father loves Jesus so much that He shares with Jesus His innermost secrets concerning His plan for mankind. Guess what? *You* have a right to know God's secrets concerning His plans (1 Corinthians 2:9-10, *AMP*). Now isn't this an incentive to make living for your heavenly Father a priority?

The "New" You

The moment you believed that Jesus Christ is the Son of God, accepted the work that He did for you on the cross and began living for God was the moment you became born again. How can a person be "born again"? Can he or she reenter his or her mother's womb and be reborn? Nicodemus, a Pharisee, or religious leader of Jesus' day, asked Him the same questions (John 3:1-5). Jesus' response was that being born again involves a *spiritual* rebirth. No one can reenter his or her mother's womb. Instead, your spirit is the part of you that is reborn or recreated. Man is a three-part being; he is spirit (made in the image of God), soul (the place where your mind, will and emotions reside) and body (the "house"). In simple terms, you are a *spirit* who possesses a *soul* and lives in a *body* (1 Thessalonians 5:23).

The Bible says, *"...if any man be in Christ, he is a new creature: old things are passed away; behold, all things are become new* (2 Corinthians 5:17). *The Amplified Bible* says that the previous moral and spiritual condition of any person who is in Christ is no longer an issue. To be *in Christ* simply means that the slate has been wiped clean and that you have entered a new life with and because of

Jesus (1 Corinthians 15:22). For example, when you were born into the world, you were given a name. With that name you received an identity. Likewise, when you are *born again*, you decide to leave the state and life of sin that you were accustomed to and receive a new spiritual identity. It is similar to being in a witness protection program where your old identity is "destroyed," and you obtain a new one.

You are now a new specie of being that has never before existed. The "old" you who was *in* Adam and *in* sin, has been replaced by the "new" you. You no longer live in a sinful state of being as Adam and all the rest of mankind did after he sinned. Your rebirth was a birth into the family of God. You have been "saved."

John 3:17 says, *"For God sent not his Son into the world to condemn the world but that the world through him might be saved."* Being "saved" means more than just having a ticket out of hell and into heaven. A simple definition of *save* is "to keep safe and sound; to rescue from danger or destruction; to save a suffering one (from perishing); to make well; to heal; to restore to health." The word *salvation* comes from the Greek word *soteria,* which is translated "deliverance from slavery and sin; preservation of life and physical health; pardon; restoration; liberation from restraint." All this and more are a part of the "salvation package" you received when you became born again.

You no longer *have to* live in sin if you choose not to. You don't *have to* fear dying in a tragic accident or because of a disease. You don't *have to* live in poverty if you don't want to. You are saved and are *already* delivered from eternal damnation. That's something worth shouting about!

God saved you because He loves you. Now it's time to love Him in return by living wholeheartedly for Him—it's the least you can do. Allow your life's pursuits to be motivated by your love for Him. Love Him enough to be like Him. When others see the way you live, they should immediately recognize that God is in you. As a born-again Christian, your presence alone should demand an explanation to the point where others will want to know the God you serve. After all, that's what Christianity is all about!

Chapter 2
Forgiven and Free

2

~

Forgiven and Free

Many new and "veteran" Christians find it difficult to live wholeheartedly for God. More often than not, this is a result of the shame they feel because of their past sins. Some ask, "How can God use me when I have done so many bad things?" Each of us, at one time or another, has asked this question. We have questioned whether or not we are really born again and how a loving God could love sinners. Surely He has some restrictions on His love, doesn't He?

This would be true if God's love was conditional, but it's not. He has committed Himself to loving us *despite* our sins. Let's not forget what Romans 5:8 says: *"But God commendeth his love toward us, in that, while we were yet sinners, Christ died for us."* Did you get that? He loved us when we were sinners. That's right—even when we were doing all kinds of deceitful, hateful and hurtful things. He saw us, but He loved us *anyway*.

Our past, present and future sins are not a problem to God. He took care of the sin problem thousands of years ago when Jesus died to set us free from bondage to sin and death. In fact, now that we are born again, God no longer sees us as sinners.

It has been a popular thing for some Christians to refer to themselves as "sinners saved by grace." Numerous songs have been written with this unscriptural message. Nowadays, you can hardly turn on the Gospel radio station without hearing someone singing about their sins and how unworthy they are of God's love. The truth is that either you are a sinner *or* someone who is saved by grace—you can't be both. A *sinner* is "someone who *practices* sin." He or she can't help but to live that way, because he or she is in a state of sin. For example, a caterpillar will remain a caterpillar until it goes through the process of becoming a butterfly.

Likewise, we are no longer sinners, because we have gone through the process of becoming born-again. A person who is *not* born again does not have the life of Christ and is consequently bound to a life of sin. Sinners *sin* because that's what sinners do. Therefore, it stands to reason that as born-again believers, we should *live* like we've been given new life. It makes no sense to wear the title, but not live the life.

As believers, we shouldn't hold on to the past. God said, *"Remember ye not the former things, neither consider the things of old. Behold, I will do a new thing; now it shall spring forth…"* (Isaiah 43:18-19). What things from your past are you holding on to? Yes, you may have done some terrible things—things that hurt others, hurt you and for which you haven't yet forgiven yourself.

Listen. No one is perfect; we *all* make mistakes. It's how we *recover* from our mistakes that is important. You can either pity yourself for the things that you have done, or you can move forward with your life and stand firm in the fact that God loves you regardless.

A Commitment to Forgive

Nothing that you could ever do will make God love you any less. Think of the worst thing that you have ever done. Guess what? Even *that* doesn't stop Him from loving you. What I love about the Lord is that He committed Himself to loving us *before* we were ever born.

Ephesians 1:4, in *The Amplified Bible,* is a powerful scripture which says, *"Even as [in His love] He chose us [actually picked us out for Himself as His own] in Christ before the foundation of the world, that we should be holy (consecrated and set apart for Him) and blameless in His sight, even above reproach, before Him in love."* God handpicked you before you were born so that you could live for Him. Why did He do it? Because of His love for you. Therefore, despite your shortcomings, rest assured that God is still forgiving. And because He is forgiving, why not learn to forgive yourself? Love yourself enough to let go of the past and enjoy your new life in Jesus Christ!

No More Sin-Consciousness

Forgiving yourself may not be easy, especially when you are continually conscious of your sins. Since the moment you became born again, have you ever sinned and not felt worthy enough to pray, read the Bible or attend church? Perhaps you felt ashamed and thought, *I don't deserve to pray and get answers from God because I've sinned against Him.* Instead of "feeling" worthy of God's love, you felt guilty. And the more guilt you felt, the more difficult it became to "get back on track," so to speak.

Most people who experience this have what the Bible calls *sin consciousness* (Romans 3:20, *AMP*). In other words, they have a guilty conscience and are constantly reminded of their faults. They feel that they'll never be free from sin and will never be able to do what's required to live sin-free. They are continually asking God to forgive them. They wake up asking for His forgiveness just in case they sinned while they were asleep! This may sound humorous, but there are a lot of people who live that way.

I am not suggesting that you shouldn't *acknowledge* that you have sinned when it happens. The Bible says, *"If we confess our sins* [to God], *he* [God] *is faithful and just to forgive us our sins, and to cleanse us from all unrighteousness* [sin; wrong-standing]. *If we say that we have not sinned, we make him a liar, and his word is not in us"* (1 John 1:9-10).

My point is that you should not be so conscious of your sins that you hinder yourself from enjoying life. I know people who are stuck in "I'm a sinner" mode and are not enjoying their life in Christ. They beat themselves up for making mistakes and are afraid to do anything constructive with their lives. Don't allow this to be the case with you!

When you make a decision to stop thinking that you're a good-for-nothing sinner and instead begin focusing on the fact that God is a forgiving God, you won't have a problem receiving His forgiveness. His willingness to forgive you is not based on what *you* do, per se, but rather on what Ephesians 1:7 and Colossians 1:14 say: You have redemption and the forgiveness of sins because *Jesus* (not anyone else) shed His blood on the cross.

Your Right to Be Forgiven

To fully grasp what Jesus did for you, you must understand the role of a high priest under the Old Testament, or old covenant, law. There is a connection between Jesus' mission on the earth and that of a high priest. The high priest was appointed to stand before God on behalf of the Jews. Think of him as a go-between, or a middleman, who sacrificed animals annually as a sin offering for his own sins and the sins of the people (Hebrews 7:27; 9:6-7). The animals symbolically took on the sins of God's people so that they would not have to bear the burden of sin themselves (Leviticus 15:15).

The problem with the yearly sacrifice was that it merely *covered* the sins; it did not wipe them away. When something is covered, it still exists; it's just not in plain sight. Although God accepted the annual sacrifice, it was only a *temporary* solution to a far-reaching problem (Hebrews 10:1-4).

Remember that when Adam sinned against God, it

affected the entire world, including the universe and heaven (Romans 5:12-14). The effects of sin spread from the lowest region of hell up to, but not including, the throne of God and everywhere in between. He, therefore, had to institute a plan that would take care of the sin problem for good. That is where Jesus came into play. Hebrews 9:23-28 in *The Amplified Bible* tells us that Jesus had to cleanse the "patterns," or instruments of worship, in God's temple in heaven with His own blood. The earthly temples that were built by men were only replicas of the heavenly temple that God Himself built.

As God's High Priest, Jesus was the only One Who could cleanse heaven's temple for good. First Timothy 2:5 says, *"For there is one God, and **one mediator between God and men,** the man Christ Jesus...."* What the priests under the old covenant could not accomplish through animal sacrifices, Jesus took care of *once and for all* through His own death. The blood that was shed by those animals was limited in what it could do for man's sins (Hebrews 10:1-4). The Bible says that God anointed (empowered) and ordained (appointed) Jesus to be the *last* and *final* High Priest for mankind (Hebrews 4:14-16; 6:19-20; 7:22-27).

Not only was Jesus the ultimate High Priest of God, He also became the ultimate sacrificial lamb. Revelation 13:8 says He was *"...the* Lamb ***slain** from the foundation of the world."* John the Baptist said, *"...Behold the Lamb of God, which taketh away the sin of the world"* (John 1:29). Jesus took the sins of everyone—past, present and future—and received them into His own body while on the cross.

Isaiah 53 paints a vivid picture of how this happened. According to verses 4-5 in *The Amplified Bible*:

> Surely He has borne our griefs (sicknesses, weaknesses, and distresses) and carried our sorrows and pains [of punishment]...He was wounded for our transgressions, He was bruised for our guilt and iniquities; the chastisement [needful to obtain] peace and well-being for us was upon Him, and with the stripes [that wounded] Him we are healed and made whole.

Did Jesus *really* have to shed His blood for our forgiveness? You had better believe it! The Bible says *"...everything is purified by the means of blood, and without the shedding of blood there is neither release from sin and its guilt nor the remission of the due and merited punishment for sins"* (Hebrews 9:22, *AMP*).

When you ask for God's forgiveness, He doesn't keep your sins on file just in case you mess up in the future. According to Isaiah 43:25 and Hebrews 10:17, He chooses to forget about your sins for good! He won't waste His time reviewing your "criminal record" in the great courtroom of heaven just to hold it against you. In fact, according to Him, you don't have a record. You may think that He's ready to sentence you to a life of struggle and suffering the moment you sin, but that is not His nature. In fact, the Bible's message is very clear: God *loves* you and wants the best for you (Jeremiah 29:11; John 3:16).

Although you may not feel lovable in light of your past, remember that God loves you and is ready to forgive you regardless of what you have done—even if others are not. When you sin, your job is to quickly ask for forgiveness and repent, or stop committing that sin for good. *Repentance* is not saying, "God, I'm sorry." That's remorse. Instead, repentance involves your making a quality decision not to sin anymore. Making that decision is a key to living a sin-free lifestyle.

There is a bumper sticker that reads, "Christians aren't perfect. They're just forgiven." How true it is. You may not be perfect, but God gave you the right to be forgiven. As far as He is concerned, forgiveness wipes the slate clean and makes you His forever! Now isn't that an awesome benefit of being born again?

Chapter 3
Reigning as Royalty
(Right–Standing With God)

3

~

Reigning as Royalty
(Right-Standing With God)

Imagine what it would be like if we had to stand trial for every sin we ever committed. From the "little white lies" to adultery, fornication, slander, murder and so on, the penalties would be endless. We would probably have to serve multiple life sentences without parole just for the sins we *knowingly* committed.

When you don't have an understanding of God's love and forgiveness, it's easy to feel guilty all the time. When that's the case, you may feel that God *should* punish you. After all, punishment is needed to keep you living sin-free and holy, right? No. This false assumption is why many people perceive sickness and poverty as God's way of teaching them a lesson. Heaven will never become "bankrupt" and resort to using the Devil's tactics to get a point across to you. You can count on that.

Diplomatic Immunity in Christ

As a born-again believer, you are now exempt from having to *earn* God's forgiveness. Your exemption is a benefit of your new identity in Christ. Romans 3:19-20 in *The Amplified Bible* helps you to understand this concept:

Now we know that whatever the Law says, it speaks to those who are under the Law, so that...all the world may be held accountable to God. For no person will be justified (made righteous, acquitted, and judged acceptable) in His sight by observing...the Law. For [the real function of] the Law is to make men recognize and be conscious of sin....

The "Law" referred to here is the *Law of Moses* (the Books of Leviticus, Numbers and Deuteronomy), which prescribed specific rituals and rules by which the Israelites had to live (Exodus 24:12; Romans 10:5). It described how they had to worship God and also how to compensate for their sins through animal sacrifices and other means. As Romans 3:20 points out, the purpose of the Law was to make people sin conscious. It was established as a constant reminder that the Israelites had to live clean lives to be cleansed of their sins and receive God's forgiveness. It basically said, "Live by these Rules and you'll be on good terms with God."

Born-again believers have *already* been granted right-standing status with God, but not because of Moses' Law. Acts 13:39 in *The Amplified Bible* says, "...through [Jesus] everyone who believes [who acknowledges Jesus as his Savior and devotes himself to Him] is absolved (cleared and freed) from every charge from which he could not be justified and freed by the Law of Moses and given right-standing with God." To be justified means "to be declared righteous or in right standing" with God. To be *righteous* means "to stand before God without the sense of guilt or inferiority, as if sin never existed." God declares you righteous the moment you become born again. He also clears you of every charge that has ever been brought against you by the Devil (Colossians 2:14).

Satan's job is to accuse you of sin and justify why you should be condemned (Revelation 12:10). He's like a prosecuting attorney seeking your spiritual "death penalty." However, when the Lord declares you righteous, the charges are dropped! Satan will try to produce compelling evidence against you, but his evidence is inadmissible in God's courtroom.

You have a heavenly Defense Attorney Who has *never* lost a case. The Word of God says that Jesus is your Advocate, constantly pleading your case before God (Romans 8:34; 1 John 2:1-2). His argument is, *"Father, this is my brother (or sister) in faith. He (or she) no longer has the right to die because of his (or her) sins. I took care of that by paying his (or her) ransom with My blood."*

When Satan tries to remind you of your sins (and believe me, you'll know when he does), remind *him* of the blood that Jesus shed on the cross. He'll definitely bring up your past, but you can remind him of his future (Revelation 20:7-10)! Don't allow him to harass you. You are the righteousness of God, and righteous people *must* exercise their rights. In this case, your right is the forgiveness of sin and the right to fully enjoy the benefits of your salvation.

Because of the blood of Jesus, God always rules in your favor. Your life is no longer the Devil's business; it's God's. Therefore, when you sin, don't feel guilty. Repent and stand firm in your righteousness. Remember, God is faithful and just to forgive you (1 John 1:9).

Free to Sin?

You may ask, "What happens if I sin? Do I lose my right-standing with God?" No. Jesus paid the ultimate price with His blood to keep you in right-standing with the Father. It forever guarantees your freedom (Hebrews 10:10-14). It's like having a lifetime membership to your favorite fitness center. You have unlimited access to all that God has in store for you—wholeness in every area of your life, free of charge.

Please understand that your righteousness does *not* give you a license to sin (Romans 6:1-2). Think of it this way: Believers are not looking for a way *to* sin, but for a way *out of* sin. First Corinthians 15:34 says, *"Awake to righteousness, and sin not…."* In other words, become fully aware of and apply the principles of true righteousness so that you can refrain from sinning.

Continuing in sin doesn't cancel your righteousness; however, it does enslave you to its consequences and hinders you from experiencing God's best for you. The Bible says,

"Everything is permissible (allowable and lawful) for me; but not all things are helpful (good for me to do,

expedient and profitable when considered with other things). Everything is lawful for me; but I will not become a slave of anything or be brought under its power" (1 Corinthians 6:12, AMP).

Righteousness by Faith

Simply knowing the definition of what it means to be righteous and the fact that it isn't profitable for you to continue in sin is only half the battle. You must also *receive* your righteousness. Romans 3:22 says, *"...the righteousness of God **by faith** of Jesus Christ unto all and upon all that **believe**...."* This scripture states that righteousness is available to everyone, but it is only *received* by those who have *faith* (confidence and trust) in Jesus. In Philippians 3:8-10, the Apostle Paul said:

*Yea doubtless, and I count all things but loss for the excellency of the knowledge of Christ Jesus my Lord: for whom I have suffered the loss of all things, and do count them but dung, that I may win Christ, And be found in him, **not having mine own righteousness, which is of the law, but that which is through the faith of Christ,** the righteousness which is of God by faith: That I may know him, and the power of his resurrection, and the fellowship of his sufferings, being made conformable unto his death.*

Think of faith as your *righteousness connector—the* bridge you must cross to reach your right standing with God. By crossing that bridge, you wake up to your righteousness. Righteousness is God's *gift* to us (Romans 5:16-19). You cannot earn it by "living right" or by doing good deeds, but by faith. If living right were the only requirement for becoming righteous, then it would be tempting for you to claim that *you* made yourself righteous. Attending church, tithing, singing in the choir, having Sunday afternoon fish fries, donating money to your favorite charities or even helping the homeless doesn't make you righteous. You may be a good person, but good without God doesn't count!

The Bible says that it is *God* Who makes you righteous through His declaration (Romans 5:19). Simply put, you are righteous because God *said* so. All that you have to do is *receive*, or accept, your new state of righteousness. When you heard about God and what He did through Jesus, you believed and made Him Lord over your life. Romans 10:10 says that with your heart you believed and received the life of Christ, thereby accepting His righteousness. It also says that you confessed your faith in Christ with your mouth and received salvation.

It is also important to know that faith is more than just believing. For example, a person may believe that God loves him or her, but may not have faith in His ability to forgive him or her of sins. *True faith* involves having *confidence* in and *applying* to your life what you learn from the Word of God; in this case, it would be an application of the truth about living as the righteousness of God. You became born again by applying the principles of becoming born again. This holds true for everything else in the Word—healing, financial prosperity, you name it. I am a firm believer that *application* equals *manifestation.* When you discover a promise from God in His Word, find out what you have to do for that promise to come to pass in your life. That's exercising faith. You do what God tells you to do through His Word.

That's how righteous people live. We make a commitment to obey God's Word and live by faith, because it pleases Him (Hebrews 11:6). We trust Him and allow Him to direct us down the path of righteousness, which is the path to pleasing Him in everything that we do. Righteousness involves living a life of faith; therefore, our lives should be governed by the principles of faith. The Bible says that the *"just shall live by faith"* (Habakkuk 2:4; Romans 1:17; Galatians 3:11; Hebrews 10:38). Who are the just? Those of us who are born again and have been "declared righteous" by God.

God Pleasers Reign Supreme

The declaration of our righteousness is also a declaration that we are royalty in God's sight. First Peter 2:9 says, *"...ye are a chosen generation, a **royal priesthood,** an holy nation, a peculiar people; that ye should shew forth the praises of him who hath called you out of darkness into his marvellous light."* In simple terms, we were chosen to be King's kids, which means that we are entitled to the best that God has to offer.

We are entitled to eternal life in heaven, material

comfort on earth, divine health, peace and many other benefits. Not only that, we are *supposed* to reign as kings in life:

> *"For if because of one man's trespass (lapse, offense) death reigned through that one, much more surely will those who receive [God's] overflowing grace (unmerited favor) and the free gift of righteousness [putting them into right standing with Himself] reign as kings in life through the one Man Jesus Christ (the Messiah, the Anointed One)" (Romans 5:17, AMP).*

We are a royal body of kings who have dominion in the earth and reign with the support of heaven. The Devil no longer has dominion over us because we have been crowned with God's authority. That authority gives us the right to experience God's goodness without having to earn it and without hindrance from Satan. We don't have to accept sickness, poverty or insufficiency as a part of lives. Our authority in Christ gives us the right to prosper in every area of life. I call this *total life prosperity— prospering* physically, spiritually, mentally, socially and economically.

In addition, we were *chosen* to be priests and ambassadors of Christ in the earth. As His representatives, our lifestyles should attract others and cause them to want to know God personally. Our lives should be testimonies of how good He is to us. While the world seems to get darker and more troubling, our lives should shine brighter every day. In the midst of stock market crashes, wars, famines and other disturbing situations, we shouldn't be moved—

we shouldn't become stressed and be driven to the brink of suicide. We are the righteousness of God and we should handle life differently from the way unbelievers do. Why? Because our trust is in God, not in ourselves or in society and its way of doing things. Our trust is in His fail-proof system of prosperous living.

Think Victory!

Prospering in the things of God is a mindset. You must settle the fact that as the righteousness of God, you should not live beneath your privileges. Never get to the point of accepting "life as it is" or thinking, *This is as good as it gets.* No! You have been given the power to win big in life—in everything that you do. You must change the way you think in order to change the way you live. The Bible says that you are who you *think* you are (Proverbs 23:7). If you *think* you're defeated, then you are. If you *think* you'll "never make ends meet," then you won't.

The following poem has encouraged me over the years and has helped me to always maintain a positive attitude:

If you think you are beaten, you are.
If you think you dare not, you won't.
If you like to win, but don't think you can, it's almost a
cinch you won't.

If you think you'll lose, then you've lost.
For out in the world you'll find success begins with a
fellow's will.
It's all in a state of mind.

If you think you're outclassed, you are.
You've got to think higher to rise.
You've got to be sure of yourself before you can win a
prize.
Think big and your deeds will grow.
Think small and you'll fall behind.
Think that you can, and you will.
It's all in a state of mind.

Life's battles don't always go to the stronger, faster
man,
But sooner or later the man who wins is the fellow who
thinks he can.
For as a man thinketh in his heart, so is he.
You've got to think higher to rise.
You've got to be sure of yourself before you can win a
prize.

−Author Unknown

As you can see, how you think is *very* important. That is why the Bible encourages you to "renew your mind," or change the way you think (Romans 12:2). Now that you are born again and have been made the righteousness of God, it is vital that you begin thinking in line with God's Word. Think of it as "brainwashing." You must flush out your old way of thinking and begin thinking righteous thoughts.

Renewing your mind involves more than just thinking positively. It requires that you fully accept the Bible as God's inerrant Word. Despite what other religions teach, the Bible is God's *final* and *only* authority on how we should live. This is a bold statement, but consider what 2 Timothy 3:16-17 says: *"All scripture is given by inspiration of God, and is profitable for doctrine, for reproof, for correction, for instruction in righteousness: That the man of God may be perfect, thoroughly furnished unto all good works."*

As you can see, the Bible is designed to teach you how to live as the righteousness of God so that you can perfect your Christian walk. Therefore, commit yourself to diligently studying and applying the Word of God to your life, and you will never go wrong. Living by the Word is your ticket to enjoying the full benefits of your new life in Christ. I challenge you to make appropriating the principles of God's Word into your life a priority. As you do, be prepared to experience awesome results that will inspire others to want to live for Christ as well!

Chapter 4
Follow the Instructions

4

Follow the Instructions

Have you ever tried to use a new piece of equipment or to assemble furniture without using the instructions? You *may* have been able to figure out how it was supposed to work or how to put it together, but you more than likely found yourself fumbling around for hours with nothing to show for it. Regardless of whether it's a piece of equipment or furniture, you are always provided with a manufacturer's handbook or owner's guide to show you how it works or looks, help you avoid mishaps, save you time and keep you from becoming frustrated.

Likewise, the Bible is God's "manufacturer's handbook," given to you for your use, edification, guidance and victory. Following this handbook for life will enable you to do more than just wear the title of "Christian." Your willingness to read, study and obey the instructions outlined in the Bible will get things "working right" in your life. That's one way to determine for yourself whether or not the Word of God is authentic. It's all about *results*. Applying the Word to your life will produce positive results.

The entire section of Psalm 119 describes the importance of the Word of God. For example, verse 9 in *The Amplified Bible* says, *"How shall a young man cleanse his way? By taking heed and keeping watch [on himself] according to Your word [conforming his life to it.]"* The evidence that you are committed to living for God is your decision to conform your life to what the Bible teaches.

To live "right" means that you must live by the Word. So many people attempt to do the right thing but fail because they choose to live according to their own rules. God never intended for you to become a Christian and struggle to live the life. His vision of how you should live is clearly spelled out in His Word. As humans, we often create our own challenges to living righteously.

Take the Ten Commandments for example (Exodus 20). God did not share them with Moses and the Israelites to lord over them as a tyrant. He never said, "Thou shalt not...or else I'll pop you!" Instead, the Ten Commandments were given out of *love* for His people. Think about it. The reason why God said, "Thou shalt not kill" in verse 13 is that love *gives life*; it does not murder. Remember that God is love (1 John 4:16) and Love wants the best for everyone. Love doesn't have to commit adultery, because love for your spouse should compel you to remain faithful. Why steal when God is your *only* Source for whatever you need? He loves you too much not to provide for your needs (Philippians 4:19).

I could go on and on, but the fact is that you should develop a love for God's Word. When you do, you won't have a problem conforming to what it says. The problems that many believers face can easily be resolved by making a decision to follow the instructions found in the Word. There is not one subject that the Bible doesn't have an answer for. There are many principles that can be applied to whatever situation you may encounter. From proper eating habits and relational guidelines to financial management, the Bible deals with it all. Knowing this, however, won't do you any good if you don't take the time to *read* what the Word has to say.

Principles to Live By

At this point I would like to share several principles concerning the Word of God that will help you to mature spiritually. These principles will assist you in grounding your faith in the Word.

The Word of God:

1. Is eternal (Isaiah 40:8; 1 Peter 1:25).

2. Is spiritual "food" to nourish and assist in spiritual growth (Matthew 4:4; Psalm 119:103; Jeremiah 15:16; 1 Peter 2:2).

3. Is divinely inspired for the believer's benefit (2 Timothy 3:16; 2 Peter 1:19).

4. Is powerful and analyzes the heart (Hebrews 4:12).

5. Teaches believers how to prosper and have good success (Joshua 1:8).

6. Teaches believers how to live pure lives (Psalm 119:9; John 15:3; 2 Timothy 2:19-22).

7. Was written with a purpose (John 20:31; Romans 15:4; 1 John 5:13).

As you can see, the Bible is a very important tool—there is nothing like it. I encourage you to invest in a Bible if you don't already own one. There are many brands on the market, including online Bibles that you can use to locate and cross reference scriptures. There are also all sorts of study aides, such as concordances and atlases to assist you in learning more about the Word of God.

Spirit and Life

What also sets the Bible apart from all other books is the power behind it. There is a reason why it's been a bestseller for thousands of years. No other book in the world can change your life like the Word of God can. Jesus said, *"…The words (truths) that I have been speaking to you are spirit and life"* (John 6:63, *AMP*). In other words, His Word has a spiritual origin and is life-giving. It can also profit you in every area of your life, including your spiritual growth.

Life as we know it and the entire universe were created by the spoken Word of God and confirmed by His *written* Word:

"In the beginning was the Word, and the Word was with God, and the Word was God. The same was in the beginning with God. All things were made by him

[the Word]; and without him [the Word] was not any thing made that was made. In him [the Word] was life; and the life was the light of men" (John 1:1-5).

Did you know that you were born again because God declared His Word over your life? The light, or understanding, of His Word compelled you to get saved. First Peter 1:22-23 says,

Seeing ye have purified your souls in obeying the truth through the Spirit [of God] unto unfeigned [sincere] love of the brethren, see that ye love one another with a pure heart fervently: Being born again, not of corruptible seed, but of incorruptible, by the word of God, which liveth and abideth for ever.

In simple terms, you're a child of the Word and thereby have an obligation to love others based on what the Word says.

With this in mind, reread John 1:1-5 and replace "Word" with "Love." It's safe to do so because verse 1 says that God and His Word are one. It also stands to reason that the Person Love (God) has made Himself known through His Word. Therefore, John 1:1-5 can read,

In the beginning was [Love], and [Love] was with God, and [Love] was God. The same was in the beginning with God. All things were made by [Love]; and without [Love] was not any thing made that was made. In [Love] was life; and the life was the light of men.

That's powerful isn't it?

Obedient to Love

To live for God by living according to His Word is to express your love toward Him. It's an expression of your gratitude for His making you "new" and adopting you into His family. You should count it as an honor to live by the Word of God. He could have saved you and left you without clear instructions on how to live and prosper, but He didn't.

I can't understand why some Christians even consider turning their backs on God and returning to their old ways of living. I cannot imagine living without God. All hell breaks loose when you are separated from Love Himself. Nothing goes right when you attempt to live according to your own rules, rather than according to His Word.

Satan learned this the hard way when he rebelled against God. According to Isaiah 14:12-23, he allowed arrogance to get the best of him. In today's terminology, he thought he was "all that," but his pride became his downfall (Luke 10:18). Satan's rebellion was an uprising against God and His Word. In fact, it was a *rejection* of God's love.

The Devil would love to con you into rebelling against God, just as he did Adam and Eve. He uses the power of suggestion to cause people to doubt God and His Word. Once you doubt the Word, Satan has you right where he wants you. He'll try to weaken your faith and strengthen your fears. When that happens, it won't be long before you completely reject God and, ultimately, His love.

Don't allow this to happen to you! Discipline yourself to read God's Word daily. Start by studying scriptures that discuss the love of God. Ground yourself in the knowledge of Who He is and how much He loves you. It's like driving a telephone pole deep into the ground to keep it from falling over. Likewise, ground your faith in God's love by depositing the Word in your heart and mind so deep that you won't ever doubt Him.

When Satan applies pressure to your life to force you to quit, apply what I call "faith pressure" until *he* gives up. Faith pressure involves a firm commitment not to crumble under the Devil's pressure. Faith pressure involves praying, reading the Word and diligently living by the Word of God come "hell or high water." Simply put, it requires backbone and tenacity!

Chapter 5
Plugged Into the Source

5

Plugged Into the Source

There is nothing like a good understanding of the Bible. Once you comprehend it, you can begin to apply its principles to your life. A clear understanding of the Word will also show you that God will never leave you (1 Kings 8:57). That may seem strange, especially since God is in heaven and you are on earth; however, that is where the Holy Spirit comes in.

When you became born again, God supernaturally placed His Spirit within you. He did this to make you a "new creation" in Christ (2 Corinthians 5:17). That's what it means to be "born again." You "die to," or turn away from, your old ways of doing things and are "resurrected into," or take on, *God's ways* of doing things. Ezekiel 36:26-27 says:

> *A new heart also will I give you, and a new spirit will I put within you: and I will take away the stony heart out of your flesh, and I will give you an heart of flesh. And I will put my spirit within you, and cause you to walk in my statutes, and ye shall keep my judgments, and do them.*

By your "giving" your heart to the Lord, you gave Him the opportunity to give you *His*. And by God's infusing your spirit with His, He was able to share *Himself* with you.

According to 1 Corinthians 2:9-12, all that makes up Who God is and all that you have a right to, has been revealed to you by His Spirit. That includes knowing and receiving His love and the ability to develop His character (Romans 5:5).

He Is a Person

Since becoming born again, have you realized that you don't have the same "taste" for ungodly things like you used to? That's because you have "tasted" the goodness of God through a spiritual connection with Him through the Holy Spirit (Psalm 34:8). There may have been a time when you would sin and not feel *convicted*—in other words, it didn't bother you. But things are different now that you're saved. Some people say that when you become born again, "you don't stop dancing, you just change partners." I like that!

You may have gotten into a lot of trouble with the partners with whom you used to associate in the past. But God has sent you a new Holy Partner to live in you—His Holy Spirit. Jesus told His disciples that God would send them another Comforter just like Him (John 14:26). *The Amplified Bible* expounds on the Holy Spirit's role as a Comforter. It tells us that He is a Counselor, Helper,

Intercessor, Advocate, Strengthener and Standby. He is also a Teacher Whose job it is to teach you everything there is to know about God and His love.

Jesus instructed His disciples to *"...wait for the promise of the Father...For John* [the Baptist] *truly baptized with water; but ye shall be baptized with the Holy Ghost* [or Spirit] *not many day hence"* (Acts 1:4-5). This "baptism" of the Holy Spirit had nothing to do with being submerged in water. Instead, Jesus was referring to the *spiritual* infusion of God's Spirit with the spirit of those who become born again.

Guaranteed Divine Direction

The Holy Spirit is available to help you to develop a clear understanding of the truth of God's Word. He teaches you how to fellowship with the Father through prayer and how to overcome obstacles. Without the Holy Spirit, you would be without direction, focus and true companionship with God Himself. When you listen to and obey the Holy Spirit, you can minimize your chances of making mistakes, thereby maximizing your ability to succeed in life.

John 16:13 says that the Holy Spirit guides you toward God's will for your life. He does this in various ways, including impressions, or what some people call "hunches" or "a gut feeling." When your conscience "speaks" to you, that's actually the Holy Spirit attempting to direct you. He also speaks to you through the written Word of God. If you've ever read the Bible and felt as if a certain scripture was speaking directly to you or about you, more than likely that was the Holy Spirit attempting to teach you something.

The Holy Spirit can also speak to you through others, including friends, family members, your pastor or another spiritual leader. A key to determining whether or not the Holy Spirit is speaking to you through someone is to make sure that what he or she is saying lines up with what the Word of God says. Remember, Jesus said that the Holy Spirit will guide you based on the truth of God's Word (John 15:26; 16:13). You can disregard any supposed "message from Lord" if it contradicts the written Word. God will never say anything to contradict Himself. There will never be a "new" revelation or divine insight from God that is not supported by what He has *already* revealed in His Word.

Empowered to Prosper

The Word will always be your safeguard when it comes to learning from the Holy Spirit. I can't imagine what life would be like if we didn't have the Word and the Holy Spirit to teach us. One of the biggest downsides would be that we would be powerless. What makes us different from unbelievers is that we are empowered through the indwelling presence of the Holy Spirit. Let me explain.

In Acts 1:8 in *The Amplified Bible*, Jesus told His disciples, "*...you shall receive power (ability, efficiency, and might) when the Holy Spirit has come upon you, and* *you shall be My witnesses in Jerusalem and all Judea, and in Samaria, and unto the uttermost part of the earth."* The power that is made available to you through the Holy Spirit is the ability to succeed at whatever you do.

The Secrets We Speak

There is another level of power you have access to through the Holy Spirit. As you will come to know, God doesn't keep anything concerning Himself *from* us. Instead, He keeps things in secret *for* us, for our benefit. Psalm 78:2 and Matthew 13:35 tell us that prophets speak the hidden things that have been ordained from the foundation of the world. A *prophet* is simply "someone who declares God's Word concerning past, present or future events."

The Bible says that as believers, we can speak the wisdom of God *in a mystery* for our benefit (1 Corinthians 2:7, *AMP*). When you and I confess, or declare, God's Word, we become the prophets of our own destinies. To *confess* means to "say the same thing as; to admit."

According to 1 Corinthians 2:12-13,

We have received, not the spirit of the world, but the spirit which is of God; that we might know the things that are freely given to us of God. Which things also we speak, not in the words which man's wisdom teacheth, but which the Holy Ghost teacheth....

The Holy Spirit helps us to speak hidden wisdom so that we

might know and receive what God has freely given to us.

Romans 8:26 says that the Spirit helps us in our infirmities, or weaknesses, when we pray—especially when we don't know what to pray for. He does this by praying God's perfect will through us (vv. 26-27). Verse 26 says, *"...the Spirit [Himself] maketh intercession for us with groanings, which cannot be uttered."* These "groanings" refer to the spiritual language called *tongues*, which cannot be understood solely through our human understanding. Tongues are not demonic; instead, they are a source of supernatural power that is made available to every believer.

Acts 2:1-4 tells us that on the Day of Pentecost, the disciples and other followers of Jesus were filled with God's Spirit, and they began to speak in other tongues, or languages. Remember that this represented the spiritual empowerment that Jesus promised they would receive (Acts 1:8).

First Corinthians 14:2 in *The Amplified Bible* says, *"For one who speaks in an [unknown] tongue speaks not to men but to God, for no one understands or catches his meaning, because in the [Holy] Spirit he utters secret truths and hidden things [not obvious to the understanding]."* Through speaking in tongues, the Holy Spirit is able to reveal to you the hidden truths concerning God and His way of doing things (John 16:13; 1 Corinthians 2:10).

Speaking in tongues allows you to receive God's wisdom and spiritual insight concerning situations about which you may not know. This is true even though you may not understand what you are saying. Think of speaking in tongues as the "Morse Code" that the Devil is unable to intercept. You can transmit top-secret information directly to heaven, and God will respond with the results of what you have spoken in tongues.

Taking advantage of this ability requires faith on your part. It takes faith to speak in a supernatural language that you don't understand. You must believe in your heart that you have *already* received the results of what you have prayed in tongues *before* you actually see anything manifest.

Prayer in tongues is a powerful tool and is the most secure way to withdraw wisdom and insight from God. Think of it in terms of a secured Internet connection. For example, when you make a purchase online, you don't submit your credit card information unless you're certain that the site is secured. By taking this precaution, you avoid making your credit information available to computer hackers.

In the same way that a secured site keeps your financial information safe, speaking in tongues hinders the Devil from "hacking" into your prayers and stealing answers from you. You are equipped with God's power and are able to withdraw the wisdom you need for healing, debt deliverance or the salvation of a loved one. Most importantly, speaking in tongues enables you to cultivate a more intimate relationship with God. Jude 20-21 says, *"But ye, beloved, building yourselves on your most holy faith, praying in the Holy Ghost, Keep yourselves in the love of God....*" Speaking in tongues helps you to mature spiritually and to operate in the love of God. For example, when you're tempted to be rude or to become upset for being treated rudely, try speaking in tongues. The more you do so, the less likely you will respond in an unloving manner.

The Holy Spirit's job is to speak all things that pertain to the love of God. He understands that words have the power to change situations and that there is nothing like using the power of love to make things happen.

Receive Your Gift

There is no secret ritual to perform to obtain the gift of tongues. Being born again is the only prerequisite (Acts 2:38). Although you're the one who actually speaks audibly, the Holy Spirit gives you the utterance, or the words to say. John 7:38 in *The Amplified Bible says* that living waters, or wisdom, will flow out of your innermost being, which is your human, reborn spirit. Also, another believer can pray and "lay their hands" on you as a point of contact to help you receive the gift of tongues. The laying on of hands is scriptural (Acts 8:17; 19:6); God can administer this gift to you through others.

As with any gift from God, you must receive tongues by faith. Disregard all fears concerning this gift, because fear will cause you to miss out on God's best for you. Open your mouth as an act of faith, then allow the Holy Spirit to speak through you. Although what you hear may sound strange, (like gibberish or baby talk) continue to speak as the Holy Spirit leads you.

I don't believe that speaking in tongues is a prerequisite to making it to heaven. However, it will help to "boost" your faith while you're on the earth. Speaking in tongues regularly is the key to keeping your spiritual "battery" charged. Therefore, why not take advantage of the power that has been made available to you through the Holy Spirit? It's time to plug into the Power Source that will keep you motivated to live for God for the rest of your life!

Chapter 6
Stake Your Claim!

6

Stake Your Claim!

As a born again believer, you have an inheritance that must be claimed before Jesus returns. It is part of the prosperous life that every Christian should experience right now. Money, houses, real estate, cars, promotion, good health, stress-free living and much more are included in that inheritance. Sadly, many believers are anxiously waiting until they get to heaven to enjoy this *total life prosperity*. As children of God, we are *guaranteed* an inheritance that has been set aside for us to enjoy on earth. Our born-again status qualifies us for it.

To understand the connection between being born again and your spiritual birthright, think of what it means to *inherit*: "to receive by descent from an ancestor; to take by being an heir." According to John 1:12 and Galatians 4:4-6, you are a part of God's family. Proverbs 13:22 states that a good man leaves an inheritance for his children and grandchildren. Your heavenly Father has already prepared a wonderful inheritance for you.

Romans 8:17 says that you are God's heir and a joint-heir with Christ. That means you have a right to inherit everything Jesus has a right to. In fact, *The Amplified Bible says*, "…[we are] heirs of God and fellow heirs with Christ [sharing His inheritance with Him]…" To be a joint-heir with Jesus is a privilege. Just as He was appointed the Heir and lawful Owner of *all things* according to Hebrews 1:2, you, too, have been given the same honor. As far as God is concerned, you are co-owner of the entire universe (Psalm 24:1; Psalm 115:16).

First Timothy 6:17 says that God has given believers *all things* to profusely enjoy. *The Amplified Bible says* that He "*richly and ceaselessly provides us with everything for [our] enjoyment.*" Because the Father loves us, we have a right to live as Jesus did while He was on earth. He never lacked anything. In fact, He never experienced poverty, nor did He know what it was like to live from paycheck to paycheck. If He were living on earth today, He would drive the finest cars and live in the finest houses. Are we any different from Him? No! Some may think, *Jesus is the Son of God. Of course God would meet all of His needs.* As God's children, however, we are entitled to have our needs met (Philippians 4:19).

We also benefit from the loving promise that God made to bless Abraham (Genesis 12:1-3). That "blessing" refers to an "empowerment to prosper and succeed in every area of life." As a side note, Deuteronomy 28:1-14 outlines the physical manifestation, or the result of being empowered by God, as well as your responsibility as a steward of His blessing. If you ever question whether or not you are a blessed man or woman, read these verses to remind yourself otherwise. Never forget that you are blessed and highly favored—you're God's favorite and He loves you!

How do you know that you have a right to the Father's blessing? The promise to bless Abraham included his spiritual and biological offspring. Jesus was a part of Abraham's *biological* lineage, and you are a part of his *spiritual* lineage (Galatians 3:16, 26-29). Therefore, as Abraham's heir, you should succeed in *everything* you do.

Become Inheritance-Minded

Success in the things of God comes when you're not "all talk and no game" as some Christians tend to be. In other words, some *say* they have faith in God and that they believe in His promises, but there are no results to back it up. That's just like a football player bragging about his skills on the field before a big game, but when it's game time, he can't make the plays that count!

Unfortunately, nonbelievers mock Christians when they are unable to see the tangible evidence of their faith in God. For years, we "faith people" have been ridiculed for our belief in pursuing the promises of God listed in the Bible. We have been labeled "Bible Thumpers," "Holy Rollers" and the "name it and claim it crowd." Many believers, however, have yet to claim their inheritance. More often than not, it is because they are unaware of its existence. Many have been conditioned to think that they should not expect too much from God, or that He wants them to struggle and work hard for a living. God *does not* want you to struggle another day in your life! You have a right to live comfortably and benefit from His goodness. That is why He sent Jesus—to give you the right to enjoy life.

In Luke 4:18, Jesus said,

The Spirit of the Lord is upon me, because he hath anointed me to preach the gospel to the poor; he hath sent me to heal the brokenhearted, to preach deliverance to the captives, and recovering of sight to the blind, to set at liberty them that are bruised.

In this scripture, Jesus is referring to His power to heal, deliver and set free the *brokenhearted* poor, the *captive* poor, the *blind* poor, and the *bruised* poor.

The word *gospel* is translated "good news." To be *poor* simply means "to be without" or "to be in lack." Therefore, Jesus came to preach good news to those who are without (or in lack). What is good news to a poor man? That he doesn't *have to* be poor anymore because Jesus possesses the power to deliver him from a life of poverty. A blind man doesn't *have to* remain blind; Jesus is willing and able to heal him.

Many believers accept lack and sickness in their lives because they settle for less than God's best. They are unaware of their rights. For example, you have an undeniable right to:

1. Receive answers to your prayers (Jeremiah 33:3; 1 John 5:14-15)
2. Have wealth and riches (Psalm 66:12,112:3; Proverbs 13:22)

3. Profit as an entrepreneur (Ecclesiastes 7:11; Isaiah 48:17)

4. Live in divine health (Deuteronomy 7:15; Isaiah 53:4-5; 3 John 2)

5. Heal the sick and cast out devils (Mark 16:17-18; Matthew 10:8)

6. Give birth to and raise healthy children (Deuteronomy 7:14; 28:4; Psalm 127:3-4; Isaiah 54:13)

7. God's safety and protection (Psalm 91:10-11; 103:4; Isaiah 54:14-17)

8. Raise the dead to life through God's power (Ezekiel 37:3-10; Matthew 10:8).

Because God loves you, you have an advantage over the world, which gives you the right to have more than enough to meet *your* needs *and* the needs of others. You have a right to live, eat, dress and drive better than those who don't have God in their lives. You don't have to work hard to live better. The key is to work *smarter,* not harder. To do so, you must renew your mind concerning what God desires for you.

To lay hold of, or possess, your divine inheritance, you must be more *inheritance-minded* than *need-minded.* Begin focusing more on the reality of your inheritance rather than on the reality of your needs. Inheritance-minded people believe and stand firm on the promise that God will supply all of their needs (Philippians 4:19). Need-minded Christians seldom claim their rights with

God. Instead, they complain about what they don't have or why they can't have it. They sit idly by watching others drive around in *their* cars, live in *their* houses, wear *their* clothes and spend *their* money.

The world is full of material wealth and blessings that belong to *us*. The Bible says that King Solomon was extremely wealthy (2 Chronicles 1:12). I believe his wealth still exists. If, however, you don't seize your portion, it will remain unclaimed by its rightful owner.

Get What's Yours NOW!

You must seize your inheritance like a soldier seizing prisoners of war. Your wealth has been held captive as a POW. Your job is to form a personal attack plan based on God's plan (His Word) and recover it forcefully (Matthew 11:12). Attack the life you *don't* want to live so that you can *attract* the abundant, God-kind of life you have a *right* to live (John 10:10).

First, realize that the Word of God is the creative tool that brought the entire world and everything in it into existence (John 1:1-3). Genesis 1 shows us that God spoke words when He created the world. Verses 3 through 29 say repeatedly, "And God *said*." Verse 31, however, says "And God *saw*." I believe that He *saw* the results of what He *said*. The words that He spoke were faith-filled words that possessed creative power. Remember that Hebrews 11:1-3 shows the connection between God's Word and faith: *"Through faith, we understand that the worlds were framed by the word of God..."* (verse 3). Faith, or the Word, is the spiritual material needed to construct natural, or physical, things (Hebrews 11:1). Before a house is built, for example, an idea is conceived in the mind of the architect. Blueprints are then designed, which specify the materials needed for the building project.

Likewise, the Word of God contains the idea, or blueprint, and the faith "material" for whatever it is you desire in life. Let's say you want a new house. Stake your claim by looking up scriptures such as Deuteronomy 6:11 and Nehemiah 9:25 that talk about inheriting houses; then study and confess them daily. To *confess* simply means to "admit" or "say the same thing as." Confessions *based on God's Word* affirm your confidence in His promises concerning your inheritance and the things you desire of Him.

The key to obtaining positive results is living by faith and exercising diligence. Hebrews 11:6 says that faith pleases God and that He rewards diligence. You may be tempted to quit, especially after confessing the Word and not seeing immediate results—but don't! Your harvest may be one confession away (Galatians 6:9).

It's just like being an expectant mother. Although she may not *see* signs of pregnancy during the first or second trimester, that does not mean she isn't pregnant. Likewise, when you plant the faith "seed" of God's Word in the womb of your heart, conception takes place. Your heart, or spirit, is the perfect ground to nurture the Word so that it can produce a harvest in your life. You may not see immediate signs of your healing, house, car, promotion or business; however, if you continue confessing the Word daily, a delivery *will* take place!

In addition, *do not neglect to use common sense!* For example, you have a right to divine health; however, eating unhealthy foods and not exercising regularly defeats the purpose. Instead, do whatever it takes to learn how to maintain physical health while you are maintaining your spiritual health. The same is true for financial prosperity. It does you no good to confess that you are out of debt when you make unnecessary credit card purchases because you lack self-control or the ability to distinguish a need versus a want.

Another key to receiving your inheritance is living a holy lifestyle; God requires it (Leviticus 19:2). Holiness, however, has nothing to do with your hairstyle or the clothes you wear. Just because a person can quote a ton of scriptures doesn't make him holy. Wearing makeup doesn't make you less holy; neither does wearing a burlap dress make you holy. True *holiness* involves living by the standards that have been set down in God's Word. You must comply with whatever it says—no questions asked. Why? Because it is the final authority by which every believer must live. Holiness simply says, "I love the Father and I agree with Him and with what His Word says."

Living holy keeps you from sinning. Sin makes cowards of men because it affects your self-confidence. For instance, when you sin, you generally aren't in a hurry to pray and spend time with the Lord. You would probably be more concerned with your mistakes than God's willingness to forgive you. Keep in mind that sin does not stop God from loving you; in fact, nothing will (Romans 8:38-39). It certainly doesn't erase your name from His inheritance list. It will, however, damage your confidence—something Hebrews 10:5 warns against: *"Cast not away therefore your confidence, which hath great recompense of reward."*

Over the years, I have learned to trust God's Word and not waver from His promises. My confidence level has increased because He remains true to His Word. I cannot afford to stop confessing scriptures, living holy, tithing, giving offerings, blessing others and doing whatever else He tells me to do. I have invested a lot in doing things God's way, and I'm willing to do whatever it takes to ensure that I receive the results I desire.

This should be your attitude as well. No matter what challenges you face or in what situation you find yourself, remain diligent with your plan of attack. You have a large inheritance with your name on it, and nothing should stop you from claiming it!

Chapter 7
Share the Gift

7

Share the Gift

I am a firm believer that God did not save you *just* for you. In other words, your new life in Christ has a purpose—to be a witness, or testimony, of the blessing that comes from living for God. You are expected to share Jesus with unbelievers. This may sound like a big task. It may not be easy for you to share the love of God with strangers or with the people who are close to you. Keep in mind, however, that you're not expected to "share Jesus" in your own strength. Instead, you have been empowered by the Holy Spirit, Who gives you the ability to be an effective witness (Acts 1:8).

Here are several major reasons for winning souls to the kingdom or family of God.

1. Jesus was a winner of souls.

2. The harvest of unsaved people is great and the harvesters are few (Luke 10:2).

3. Winning souls is Jesus' Great Commission to believers (Mark 16:15-16).

As you can see, there is a great need to win people to

the Lord. We have the life-changing message concerning Jesus Christ, which is a message of love. Others need to know why we are committed to living for God. They need to know why we love Him. The Bible says, *"...be ready always to give an answer to every man that asketh you a reason of the hope that is in you..."* (1 Peter 3:15). Your response must be based on what the Word of God says. Not only that, your personal testimony will be a blessing to someone. I have heard it said that your testimony is the best witness. How true it is.

Live the Life, Save a Life

A major reason why others need to know how your life has been changed is so that they may be able to relate to you. Someone somewhere is living like you *used* to live and needs to know how to be set free. You probably never thought that God could use your past to change someone's life, did you?

The Apostle Paul shared with Timothy, his "spiritual son" in the ministry, the importance of being a godly example: *"Let no man despise thy youth: but be thou an example of the believers, in word, in conversation, in charity, in spirit, in faith, in purity"* (1 Timothy 4:12). Paul's instructions were for Timothy to be an example of spiritual maturity despite his age. Because of his "calling," or spiritual assignment from God, Timothy had a responsibility to effectively represent the lifestyle of a true believer in Christ.

You, too, have a responsibility to effectively represent Christ in every way. Being a good witness requires that your public and private lifestyles be aligned with the Word of God. Matthew 5:16 says that your "light," or the evidence that you are a believer, should shine bright so that others may recognize that God is in you and so that they would want to live for Him as well.

Unfortunately, not every believer is a good witness. Some are living lifestyles that are equal to or worse than sinners'. When a Christian is "straddling the fence" between living a godly and an ungodly life, his or her choice to compromise could lead others away from God rather than to Him. The Bible refers to this type of believer as "lukewarm," and God chooses not to use lukewarm Christians (Revelation 3:16).

Zealous and Directed

If you ever expect for the Father to use you to impact the lives of others, make sure that you keep His ultimate purpose in mind—to communicate His love toward the world (John 3:16). Allow this to be the motive behind everything that you do for the Lord. Motive without love is pointless!

Too many new and veteran believers go about winning souls in the wrong way. Rather than testify of God's love, they "cram the Bible down the throats" of their potential converts. It becomes a job rather than a loving mission, a drudgery rather than a tremendous exploit for God.

Christianity is not about recruiting the lost and "keeping score" of how many people you or I lead to the Lord; it's about loving people God's way!

The Apostle Paul delivered a strong message in his first letter to the Christians in the city of Corinth. In 1 Corinthians 14:12 *(AMP)*, he said that it's okay to desire to develop your spiritual gifts; however, the most important thing is that you strive to excel at doing your part to help build the kingdom of God.

When a person does not understand the love of God, it becomes difficult for him or her to effectively win others to Christ. A Christian who is zealous about the things of God but is devoid of God's love might come up with all kinds of unscriptural rules of "Christian conduct." More often than not, these kinds of believers twist what the Word says and leave others confused about certain spiritual matters. Some even cause other believers to backslide, or stop living for God. This type of Christian is dangerous, and God will hold him or her accountable for the lives they turned away from Him! In Romans 10:1-3, Paul warned the religious leaders of his day:

Brethren, My heart's desire and prayer to God for Israel is, that they might be saved. For I bear them record that they have a zeal of God, but not according to knowledge. For they being ignorant of God's righteousness, and going about to establish their own righteousness, have not submitted themselves unto the righteousness of God.

The best way to win people to God is to commit your life to exemplifying His love. The Bible says that the goodness of God, His manifested love, will lead a person to live for Him (Romans 2:4).

When you are directed by the Word of God and are motivated by His love, you won't have a problem leading others to Christ. You won't force them to accept Him; neither will you get into silly debates over what doctrine is correct. You'll be a tactful witness of God's unconditional love. Love helps you to see others through the eyes of the God of love.

One of my favorite scriptures is Proverbs 4:7: *"Wisdom is the principal thing; therefore get wisdom: and with all thy getting get understanding,"* I encourage you to ask God for wisdom on how to apply His Word to winning souls for Him. Ask to fully understand His love so that you can be like Him in every way and be an effective witness. Operating by God's wisdom, love and understanding are what will make you a true World Changer!

Conclusion

In case you would like a quick recap of this book, following are the five steps to complete salvation and the keys to receiving the Baptism of the Holy Spirit:

Complete Process of Salvation

1. Admission and recognition of sin (Psalm 51:5).

2. Repentance (1 John 1:9).

3. Confession (Romans 10:9-10).

4. Water Baptism and the Baptism of the Holy Spirit (Matthew 3:6; Acts 2:3-4,38; Acts 8:14-17).

5. Obedience to the Word of God (1 John 5:3).

Keys to Receiving the Baptism of the Holy Spirit

1. Understand that the Holy Spirit was poured out on the day of Pentecost (Acts 2:38).

2. Remember that salvation is the only qualification necessary for receiving the Baptism of the Holy Spirit (Acts 2:38).

3. Know that the laying on of hands is scriptural (Acts 8:17).

4. Dispel all fears about receiving a counterfeit spirit (Luke 11:11-13).

5. Open your mouth as act of faith to receive the Holy Spirit (Ephesians 5:18-19).

Questions & Answers

Following are a several commonly asked questions and their corresponding answers to assist you in further understanding your new life in Christ. Keep in mind that it is your responsibility to diligently study the Word of God for yourself to grow spiritually and to mature in the things of God.

1. **If I'm a new creation, why do I still have some of the same desires/compulsions?**

   Your mind is the *control center for life*. It was designed to interact with your spirit and body. When your mind is not renewed to God's Word, it will become vulnerable to all sorts of ungodly things, and those things will adversely affect your will and emotions. That is usually when you struggle between wanting to live for God and wanting to live in sin. That's when intense wicked desires overcome godly desires.

   When you became born again, only your spirit was made new. Your soul (the place where you mind, will and emotions reside) and body remained the same. Romans 12:2 says that it is important for you to renew your mind to what the Word of God says. In other words, you must change the way you think to change the way you live. The more you saturate your mind with the Word through reading, studying and, most importantly, speaking it daily, the more your ungodly

desires will be "flushed out" from your system. Second
Corinthians 10:4-5 refers to this as "pulling [down]
strongholds" of thoughts and casting them down for good.

In addition, examine your life for those things that
trigger those impulses—books, movies, magazine or
people. Once you have found them, eliminate them.
Don't continue to expose yourself to the things that
bring the worst out of you. Make a decision to only
entertain godly thoughts and desires, and set
boundaries around that decision. Every time you're hit
with an impulse to do or say something that isn't
pleasing to God, remind yourself of your boundaries
and that you love God too much to mess up!

2. **What do I do when people make fun of me or give
    me a hard time?**

No one ever said that your transition into this new life
as a Christian would be easy. Despite the criticism from
others, remain grounded in your faith. It's your
unwavering faith that will strengthen you when your
beliefs are challenged.

Jesus warned us that trouble would follow our decision
to live for Him: *"These things I have spoken unto you,
that in me ye might have peace. In the world ye shall
have tribulation: but be of good cheer; I have overcome
the world"* (John 16:33). His answer to trouble is to be
cheerful regardless of what comes our way. This may not
be easy, especially when you're accustomed to handling
situations differently. However, the implication of this

scripture is that since Jesus overcame the world and its way of doing things, you don't have a thing to worry about. In Him, or in His authority, you have the ability to overcome the world as well.

Therefore, the next time people mock you and say all kind of negative things, don't dwell on what they do and say. Allow the voice of God's Word to ring louder in your ears than their negativity. Like my wife, Taffi, says, "Don't allow anyone to 'rent space' in your mind." Your job is not to fight your own battles—it's God's (1 Samuel 17:47). Your duty is to develop the love of God and allow Jesus to live through you to the point where your adversaries will see Him in you (Galatians 2:20). Allow your example of godliness, and the benefits that come with it, to change their minds.

3. Can I keep my old friends?

If you were in boat that was sinking, would you remain in that boat even though there was a seaworthy boat next to you? Of course not! That's no different than your relationship with your old friends. Now that you are born again, you're not the same person you used to be. The "old" you is gone (2 Corinthians 5:17). As a "new" person in Christ, you should let go of anything or anyone that could potentially hinder you from living a godly lifestyle. Cutting loose of old friendships may be the best thing to do.

When you do, be tactful. Tell your friends that you're not the same person anymore. And when they question why not, use that as an opportunity to share the love of

God and lead them to salvation. They may or may not accept what you say; however, allow your life of holiness to win them over (Matthew 5:16).

4. Is it okay to have premarital sex as long as I love the person?

One of the hardest things for some believers to do is to control their sexual impulses. That's usually because they are selfish. When that happens, they have no problem compromising certain biblical principles, including the one regarding premarital sex.

The Word of God is clear on this subject: NO SEX BEFORE MARRIAGE! Throughout the Bible, premarital sex is referred to as "fornication" (Mark 7:21; Acts 15:20; Romans 1:29; 1 Corinthians 5:1; Galatians 5:19). First Corinthians 6:18 says that you must "flee" fornication—run from it! To run from sexual sin is to run from what displeases God. If you truly love God, you will love Him enough to control your body and abstain from premarital sex.

Sex is not a bad thing; it's pleasurable and designed for more than just having children. What makes intercourse beautiful and truly gratifying is when it is reserved for the institution of marriage. When you can preserve your body for the one you are supposed to marry and that person does the same, both of you can share a part of you that no one else has a right to. Sex between married couples is wonderful in God's sight.

If you've had premarital sex, don't feel condemned. Ask God to forgive you and help you to renew your mind concerning what true lovemaking is so that you can preserve yourself for your future mate. In addition, cut off any relationship that is causing you to sin against God and your body. That means no living with a boyfriend or girlfriend even if you're not having sex— the temptation to sin is too great. Instead, present your life and body to God as a living sacrifice (Romans 12:1). Remember, whatever relationship you are willing to sacrifice for the Lord, He will restore to you a hundred times better!

5. **Can I date and eventually marry someone who is not saved?**

The Word of God recommends that you should not be "…unequally yoked together with unbelievers: for what fellowship hath righteousness with unrighteousness? and what communion hath light with darkness?" (2 Corinthians 6:14). Think of being yoked to someone as being joined to someone by handcuffs—both of you have to walk together if you expect to go anywhere.

The Bible says that two people can't walk together peacefully unless they are in agreement (Amos 3:3). When a born-again Christian and an unbeliever are yoked together, their lifestyles oppose one another. One is a person who is walking toward the "light" of God, while the other is walking toward darkness. The Christian's pathway through life is illuminated by God's Word, while the sinner's pathway is darkened and leads to a dead end.

Just as oil and water don't mix but instead separate when placed in the same container, dating and eventually marrying an unbeliever could lead to separation and divorce. Now that you're saved, you are spiritually alive, but if your partner is not saved, he or she is spiritually dead. That's where problems usually come in. When you want to side with God and His Word on certain issues, such as sex, marriage, finances and attending church, your partner may devalue those issues. Again, that's what happens when one person is living in the light and can see God's instructions clearly, while the other person is oblivious to anything godly because he or she is living in darkness (1 Corinthians 2:12-15).

If you really love a person who is unsaved and believe that he or she is your future mate, pray for his or her salvation before you commit to marrying him or her. Pray that he or she will open his or her heart to the Lord. In the meantime, continue living holy and representing Christ in every way, and allow God to use your life as an example of His love. You'll be amazed at what He can do through you to lead someone to salvation.

6. Why should I be baptized in water?

Water baptism is a symbolic representation of Jesus' death, burial and resurrection. Just as He was baptized in water, so must you be baptized (Matthew 3:6). You go down into the water, carrying your "old" lifestyle and everything associated with it, with you. Water baptism is about "dying" to yourself and your old way of living so that you can begin living your "new" life for God (Romans 6:3-11). When you come up out of the water, you are forever a "new" person in Christ.

For Further Study

Resources recommended for further study (by chapter).

Chapter 1: All for Love
Lord, Teach Me How to Love
Character Development Series
Discovering Your Destiny in God

Chapter 2: Forgiven and Free
Jesus Is Our Jubilee
Living in the Power of Redemption
God-Class Living: A Teaching on Righteousness

Chapter 3: Reigning as Royalty
(Right-Standing With God)
The Image of Righteousness
Sonship: The Image of God in You
Now I Know I'm Righteous

Chapter 4: Follow the Instructions
The Divine Order of Faith
Holiness: Life in His Presence
Obedience: Your Path to Destiny

Chapter 5: Plugged Into the Source
*Hearing from God and Walking in the
   Comfort of the Holy Spirit*
Perfected Prayer
Divine Direction

Chapter 6: Stake Your Claim!

The Sins of the Mouth

How to Trouble Your Trouble

Daily Faith Confessions

Chapter 7: Share the Gift

5 Steps to Complete Salvation

So Great Salvation

How to Spend Time With God

Chapter 8: Questions & Answers

The Successful Family

S.O.S. Help! My Flesh Needs Discipline

Whose Fault Is It?: Barriers to the Blessing

Bible Reading Plan

JANUARY
01 - Genesis 1-3; Matthew 1
02 - Genesis 4-6; Matthew 2
03 - Genesis 7-9; Matthew 3
04 - Genesis 10,11; Matthew 4
05 - Genesis 12-14; Matthew 5
06 - Genesis 15-17; Matthew 6
07 - Genesis 18-20; Matthew 7
08 - Genesis 21-23; Matthew 8
09 - Genesis 24,25; Matthew 9
10 - Genesis 26-28; Matthew 10
11 - Genesis 29-31; Matthew 11
12 - Genesis 32-34; Matthew 12
13 - Genesis 35-37; Matthew 13
14 - Genesis 38-40; Matthew 14
15 - Genesis 41,42; Matthew 15
16 - Genesis 43-45; Matthew 16
17 - Genesis 46,47; Matthew 17
18 - Genesis 48-50; Matthew 18
19 - Exodus 1-4; Matthew 19
20 - Exodus 5-8; Matthew 20
21 - Exodus 9-11; Matthew 21
22 - Exodus 12,13; Matthew 22
23 - Exodus 14-16; Matthew 23
24 - Exodus 17-19; Matthew 24
25 - Exodus 20-22; Matthew 25
26 - Exodus 23,24; Matthew 26
27 - Exodus 25-27; Matthew 27
28 - Exodus 28-31; Matthew 28
29 - Exodus 32-34; Mark 1
30 - Exodus 35-37; Mark 2
31 - Exodus 38-40; Mark 3

FEBRUARY
01 - Leviticus 1-3; Mark 4
02 - Leviticus 4-6; Mark 5
03 - Leviticus 7-9; Mark 6
04 - Leviticus 10-12; Mark 7
05 - Leviticus 13-15; Mark 8
06 - Leviticus 16-19; Mark 9
07 - Leviticus 20-22; Mark 10
08 - Leviticus 23-25; Mark 11
09 - Leviticus 26,27; Mark 12
10 - Numbers 1-3; Mark 13
11 - Numbers 4-6; Mark 14
12 - Numbers 7-9; Mark 15
13 - Numbers 10-12; Mark 16
14 - Numbers 13-15; Luke 1
15 - Numbers 16-18; Luke 2
16 - Numbers 19-21; Luke 3
17 - Numbers 22-24; Luke 4
18 - Numbers 25-27; Luke 5
19 - Numbers 28-30; Luke 6-
20 - Numbers 31-33; Luke 7
21 - Deuteronomy 1-3; Luke 8
22 - Deuteronomy 4,5; Luke 9
23 - Deuteronomy 6,7; Luke 10
24 - Deuteronomy 8,9; Luke 11
25 - Deuteronomy 10,11; Luke 12
26 - Deuteronomy 12-15; Luke 13
27 - Deuteronomy 16-19; Luke 14
28 - Deuteronomy 20-22; Luke 15
29 - John 13-16

MARCH
01 - Deuteronomy 23-26; Luke 16
02 - Deuteronomy 27,28; Luke 17
03 - Deuteronomy 29-31; Luke 18
04 - Deuteronomy 32-34; Luke 19
05 - Joshua 1-3; Luke 20
06 - Joshua 4-6; Luke 21
07 - Joshua 7-9; Luke 22
08 - Joshua 10-12; Luke 23
09 - Joshua 13-15; Luke 24
10 - Joshua 16-18; John 1
11 - Joshua 19-21; John 2
12 - Joshua 22-24; John 3
13 - Judges 1-3; John 4
14 - Judges 4,5; John 5
15 - Judges 6-8; John 6

16 - Judges 9; John 7
17 - Judges 10-12; John 8
18 - Judges 13-16; John 9
19 - Judges 17-19; John 10
20 - Judges 20,21; John 11
21 - Ruth 1-4; John 12
22 - 1 Samuel 1-3; John 13
23 - 1 Samuel 4-7; John 14
24 - 1 Samuel 8-11; John 15
25 - 1 Samuel 12-14; John 16
26 - 1 Samuel 15-17; John 17
27 - 1 Samuel 18-20; John 18
28 - 1 Samuel 21-23; John 19
29 - 1 Samuel 24-26; John 20
30 - 1 Samuel 27-31; John 21
31 - 1 Chronicles 1-3; Mark 1

APRIL
01 - 1 Chronicles 4-6; Mark 2
02 - 1 Chronicles 7-10; Mark 3
03 - 2 Samuel 1-3; Mark 4
04 - 2 Samuel 4-7; Mark 5
05 - 1 Chronicles 11-13; Mark 6
06 - 1 Chronicles 14-17; Mark 7
07 - 1 Chronicles 18-20; Mark 8
08 - 1 Samuel 8-10; Mark 9
09 - 2 Samuel 11-13; Mark 10
10 - 2 Samuel 14,15; Mark 11
11 - 2 Samuel 16-18; Mark 12
12 - 2 Samuel 19-21; Mark 13
13 - 2 Samuel 22-24; Mark 14
14 - 1 Chronicles 21-23; Mark 15
15 - 1 Chronicles 24-26; Mark 16
16 - 1 Chronicles 27-29; John 1
17 - Psalm 1-6; John 2
18 - Psalm 7-10; John 3
19 - Psalm 11-15; John 4
20 - Psalm 16-19; John 5
21 - Psalm 20-24; John 6
22 - Psalm 25-29; John 7
23 - Psalm 30-34; John 8
24 - Psalm 35-38; John 9
25 - Psalm 39-43; John 10
26 - Psalm 44-48; John 11

27 - Psalm 49-53; John 12
28 - Psalm 54-58; John 13
29 - Psalm 59-63; John 14
30 - Psalm 64-68; John 15

MAY
01 - Psalm 69-72; John 16
02 - Psalm 73-76; John 17
03 - Psalm 77-79; John 18
04 - Psalm 80-84; John 19
05 - Psalm 85-89; John 20
06 - Psalm 90-94; John 21
07 - Psalm 95-99; Matthew 1
08 - Psalm 100-103; Matthew 2
09 - Psalm 104-106; Matthew 3
10 - Psalm 107-109; Matthew 4
11 - Psalm 110-113; Matthew 5
12 - Psalm 114-118; Matthew 6
13 - Psalm 119; Matthew 7
14 - Psalm 120-124; Matthew 8
15 - Psalm 125-128; Matthew 9
16 - Psalm 129-132; Matthew 10
17 - Psalm 133-136; Matthew 11
18 - Psalm 137-140; Matthew 12
19 - Psalm 141-143; Matthew 13
20 - Psalm 144-146; Matthew 14
21 - Psalm 147-150; Matthew 15
22 - 1 Kings 1,2; Matthew 16
23 - 1 Kings 3-6; Matthew 17
24 - 1 Kings 7,8; Matthew 18
25 - 2 Chronicles 1-5; Matthew 19
26 - 2 Chronicles 6-9; Matthew 20
27 - 1 Kings 9-11; Matthew 21
28 - Song of Solomon 1-3; Matthew 22
29 - Song of Solomon 4-6; Matthew 23
30 - Song of Solomon 7,8; Matthew 24
31 - Proverbs 1-3; Matthew 25

JUNE
01 - Proverbs 4-6; Matthew 26
02 - Proverbs 7-9; Matthew 27
03 - Proverbs 10-12; Matthew 28
04 - Proverbs 13-15; Luke 1
05 - Proverbs 16-18; Luke 2

06 - Proverbs 19-21; Luke 3
07 - Proverbs 22-24; Luke 4
08 - Proverbs 25-28; Luke 5
09 - Proverbs 29-31; Luke 6
10 - Ecclesiastes 1,2; Luke 7
11 - Ecclesiastes 3-5; Luke 8
12 - Ecclesiastes 6-8; Luke 9
13 - Ecclesiastes 9-12; Luke 10
14 - Job 1,2; Luke 11
15 - Job 3-5; Luke 12
16 - Job 6-8; Luke 13
17 - Job 9-11; Luke 14
18 - Job 12-14; Luke 15
19 - Job 15-17; Luke 16
20 - Job 18-21; Luke 17
21 - Job 22-24; Luke 18
22 - Job 25-28; Luke 19
23 - Job 29-31; Luke 20
24 - Job 32-35; Luke 21
25 - Job 36-39; Luke 22
26 - 1 Kings 12-14; Luke 23
27 - 2 Chronicles 10-12; Luke 24
28 - 2 Chronicles 13-15; John 1
29 - 1 Kings 15-17; John 2
30 - 1 Kings 18-19; John 3

JULY
01 - 1 Kings 21,22; John 4
02 - 2 Chronicles 17-20; John 5
03 - 2 Kings 1,2; John 6
04 - 2 Kings 3-5; John 7
05 - 2 Kings 6-8; John 8
06 - 2 Kings 9-11; John 9
07 - 2 Chronicles 21-23; John 10
08 - 2 Chronicles 24,25; John 11
09 - Joel 1-3; John 12
10 - 2 Kings 12-14; John 13
11 - Jonah 1-4; John 14
12 - Amos 1-3; John 15
13 - Amos 4-6; John 16
14 - Amos 7-9; John 17
15 - 2 Kings 15-17; John 18
16 - 2 Chronicles 26-28; John 19
17 - Hosea 1-3; John 20

18 - Hosea 4-7; John 21
19 - Hosea 8-10; Luke 1
20 - Hosea 11-14; Luke 2
21 - 2 Kings 16-20; Luke 3
22 - 2 Chronicles 29,30; Luke 4
23 - 2 Chronicles 31,32; Luke 5
24 - Micah 1,2; Luke 6
25 - Micah 3-5; Luke 7
26 - Micah 6,7; Luke 8
27 - Isaiah 1-4; Luke 9
28 - Isaiah 5,6; Luke 10
29 - Isaiah 7-9; Luke 11
30 - Isaiah 10-12; Luke 12
31 - Isaiah 13-15; Luke 13

AUGUST
01 - Isaiah 16-18; Luke 14
02 - Isaiah 19-21; Luke 15
03 - Isaiah 22,23; Luke 16
04 - Isaiah 24-27; Luke 17
05 - Isaiah 28,29; Luke 18
06 - Isaiah 30-32; Luke 19
07 - Isaiah 33-35; Luke 20
08 - Isaiah 36-39; Luke 21
09 - Isaiah 40-42; Luke 22
10 - Isaiah 43-45; Luke 23
11 - Isaiah 46-48; Luke 24
12 - Isaiah 49-51; Mark 1
13 - Isaiah 52-54; Mark 2
14 - Isaiah 55-57; Mark 3
15 - Isaiah 58-60; Mark 4
16 - Isaiah 61-63; Mark 5
17 - Isaiah 64-66; Mark 6
18 - 2 Kings 21-23; Mark 7
19 - 2 Chronicles 33,34; Mark 8
20 - 2 Chronicles 35,36; Mark 9
21 - Zephaniah 1-3; Mark 10
22 - Nahum 1-3; Mark 11
23 - 2 Kings 24,25; Mark 12
24 - Jeremiah 1,2; Mark 13
25 - Jeremiah 3-5; Mark 14
26 - Jeremiah 6-8; Mark 15
27 - Jeremiah 9,10; Mark 16
28 - Jeremiah 11,12; Matthew 1

29 - Jeremiah 13-15; Matthew 2
30 - Jeremiah 16,17; Matthew 3
31 - Jeremiah 18-20; Matthew 4

SEPTEMBER
01 - Jeremiah 21-24; Matthew 5
02 - Jeremiah 25,26; Matthew 6
03 - Jeremiah 27-29; Matthew 7
04 - Jeremiah 30,31; Matthew 8
05 - Jeremiah 32,33; Matthew 9
06 - Jeremiah 34-36; Matthew 10
07 - Jeremiah 37-39; Matthew 11
08 - Jeremiah 40-42; Matthew 12
09 - Jeremiah 43-45; Matthew 13
10 - Jeremiah 46-48; Matthew 14
11 - Jeremiah 49,50; Matthew 15
12 - Jeremiah 51,52; Matthew 16
13 - Lamentations 1,2; Matthew 17
14 - Lamentations 3-5; Matthew 18
15 - Habbakuk 1-3; Matthew 19
16 - Daniel 1,2; Matthew 20
17 - Daniel 3,4; Matthew 21
18 - Daniel 5,6; Matthew 22
19 - Daniel 7-9; Matthew 23
20 - Daniel 10-12; Matthew 24
21 - Ezekiel 1-3; Matthew 25
22 - Ezekiel 4-7; Matthew 26
23 - Ezekiel 8-11; Matthew 27
24 - Ezekiel 12-14; Matthew 28
25 - Ezekiel 15-17; Luke 1
26 - Ezekiel 18-20; Luke 2
27 - Ezekiel 21,22; Luke 3
28 - Ezekiel 23,24; Luke 4
29 - Ezekiel 25-27; Luke 5
30 - Ezekiel 28-30; Luke 6

OCTOBER
01 - Ezekiel 31,32; Luke 7
02 - Ezekiel 33-35; Luke 8
03 - Ezekiel 36,37; Luke 9
04 - Ezekiel 38,39; Luke 10
05 - Ezekiel 40,41; Luke 11
06 - Ezekiel 42-44; Luke 12
07 - Ezekiel 45,46; Luke 13

08 - Ezekiel 47,48; Luke 14
09 - Obadiah; Luke 15
10 - Esther 1,2; Luke 16
11 - Esther 3-6; Luke 17
12 - Esther 7-10; Luke 18
13 - Ezra 1-3; Luke 19
14 - Ezra 4-6; Luke 20
15 - Ezra 7,8; Luke 21
16 - Ezra 9,10; Luke 22
17 - Nehemiah 1-3; Luke 23
18 - Nehemiah 4-6; Luke 24
19 - Nehemiah 7,8; Matthew 1
20 - Nehemiah 9,10; Matthew 2
21 - Nehemiah 11-13; Matthew 3
22 - Haggai 1,2; Matthew 4
23 - Zechariah 1-3; Matthew 5
24 - Zechariah 4-6; Matthew 6
25 - Zechariah 7,8; Matthew 7
26 - Zechariah 9-11; Matthew 8
27 - Zechariah 12-14; Matthew 9
28 - Malachi 1,2; Matthew 10
29 - Malachi 3,4; Matthew 11
30 - Acts 1,2; Matthew 12
31 - Acts 3,4; Matthew 13

NOVEMBER
01 - Acts 6-8; Matthew 14
02 - Acts 9-11; Matthew 15
03 - Acts 12-14; Matthew 16
04 - Acts 15-17; Matthew 17
05 - Acts 18-20; Matthew 18
06 - Acts 21-23; Matthew 19
07 - Acts 24-26; Matthew 20
08 - Acts 27,28; Matthew 21
09 - James 1-5; Matthew 22
10 - 1 Thessalonians 1-5; Matthew 23
11 - 2 Thessalonians 1-3; Matthew 24
12 - 1 Corinthians 1-3; Matthew 25
13 - 1 Corinthians 4-6; Matthew 26
14 - 1 Corinthians 7-9; Matthew 27
15 - 1 Corinthians 10,11; Matthew 28
16 - 1 Corinthians 12-14; John 1
17 - 1 Corinthians 15,16; John 2
18 - 2 Corinthians 1-4; John 3

19 - 2 Corinthians 5-7; John 4
20 - 2 Corinthians 8-10; John 5
21 - 2 Corinthians 11-13; John 6
22 - Galatians 1-3; John 7
23 - Galatians 4-6; John 8
24 - Romans 1-3; John 9
25 - Romans 4-6; John 10
26 - Romans 7,8; John 11
27 - Romans 9-11; John 12
28 - Romans 12,13; John 13
29 - Romans 14-16; John 14
30 - Colossians 1,2; John 15

DECEMBER
01 - Colossians 3,4; John 16
02 - Philemon; John 17
03 - Ephesians 1-3; John 18
04 - Ephesians 4-6; John 19
05 - Philippians 1,2; John 20
06 - Philippians 3,4; John 21
07 - 1 Timothy 1-3; Mark 1
08 - 1 Timothy 4-6; Mark 2
09 - Titus 1-3; Mark 3
10 - Hebrews 1,2; Mark 4
11 - Hebrews 3,4; Mark 5
12 - Hebrews 5-7; Mark 6
13 - Hebrews 8-10; Mark 7
14 - Hebrews 11-13; Mark 8
15 - 1 Peter 1,2; Mark 9
16 - 1 Peter 3-5; Mark 10
17 - 2 Peter 1-3; Mark 11
18 - 2 Timothy 1-4; Mark 12
19 - Jude; Mark 13
20 - 1 John 1,2; Mark 14
21 - 1 John 3-5; Mark 15
22 - 2 John; 3 John; Mark 16
23 - Revelation 1-3; Matthew 1
24 - Revelation 4-6; Matthew 2
25 - Revelation 7-9; Matthew 3
26 - Revelation 10,11; Matthew 4
27 - Revelation 12-14; Matthew 5
28 - Revelation 15,16; Matthew 6
29 - Revelation 17,18; Matthew 7
30 - Revelation 19,20; Matthew 8
31 - Revelation 21,22; Matthew 9

About the Author

Dr. Creflo A. Dollar is the senior pastor and founder of World Changers Church International, a non-denominational Word of Faith church located in College Park, Georgia.

Formerly an educational therapist, Dr. Dollar began the ministry in 1986 with eight people. He is now an internationally known author, teacher and conference speaker with a congregation of more than 20,000 members.

Dr. Dollar has been called by God to teach the gospel with simplicity and understanding. He can be seen and heard throughout the world on the *Changing Your World* Broadcast via television and radio. He is setting the standard for excellence in ministry and making a mark that cannot be erased!

If You Would Like:

- To order books and tapes by Dr. Creflo A. Dollar

- To become a partner or supporter of Creflo Dollar Ministries

- To become an e-mail subscriber and receive the latest information concerning ministry events, new releases and special offers

- To receive a complimentary copy of *Changing Your World* Magazine

Call Us

United States and Canada ....(866) 477-7683

United Kingdom ....+44-121-359-5050

Australia ....+61-7-5528-1144

South Africa ....+27-11-792-5562

West Africa ....+234−1−270-5438

Or visit our Web site:
www.creflodollarministries.org